Old SPRINGBURN

by

ANDREW STUART

D0889455

Springburn Cross

This used to be a busy thoroughfare with a whole block of Co-op shops, offices and halls. How times have changed!! Renamed Springburn Way in 1988, the Cross is now deserted at anytime, but with new housing under construction, the place might become busier someday.

ISBN 1-872074-12-X

Broomfield Road, Springburn.

A quiet residential address occupied by doctors, ministers, teachers and prosperous publicans. This was the main entrance into Springburn Park with a wide promenade leading to the bandstand and the Winter Gardens. Such pleasures, alas, are gone. The steep descent to Balgrayhill was sealed off in the 1970s and is now stepped with handrails attached, as the modern housing around was especially built for the elderly.

INTRODUCTION

At the beginning of the 19th century, Springburn (still to be named as such) was a village community of weavers, miners, farm and quarry workers who were scattered amidst rural surroundings, linked with houses and mansions of some of Glasgow's merchants and landed gentry, situated to the north just beyond the city's boundary. By the end of that century, the village was part of Glasgow and was a vibrant working class community of some 30,000 people, housed in tenements and whose dependence was mainly upon the successful building and maintenance of railway transportation. Within the area were the workshops and repair yards of the North British Railway Co. at Cowlairs and those of the Caledonian Railway Co. at St. Rollox. There were also the locomotive building firms of Neilson, Reid & Co. at Hyde Park Works and Sharp, Stewart & Co. at the Atlas Works. Both these firms amalgamated with Dubs & Co. of Queen's Park Works in 1903 to become the North British Locomotive Co., the largest of its kind in Europe.

By 1965 the failure to adapt from steam locomotion to diesel/electric liquidated the North British Locomotive Co. and the pruning of British Railways closed the Cowlairs Workshops. At the same time, the community was being rehoused to Castlemilk, Easterhouse and overspill areas such as Cumbernauld, East Kilbride and Kirkintilloch. And thus began the demolition of Springburn in the name of urban re-development.

It is still to be proven conclusively where and when Springburn became so named. Certainly amongst the hills were many springs, burns and wells as some of the street names indicate, but the land upheavals for railway lines and housing must have covered up the Spring Burn and no map has yet shown the source.

RUSTIC BRIDGE, SPRINGBURN PARK.

Dedicated to the members of the staff of Springburn Museum Trust whose encouragement and assistance have made this book possible.

3

The Caledonian Railway Workshops were relocated from Greenock to Glasgow in 1853 and within the chosen site was the Glasgow and Garnkirk line of 1831, which terminated at Tennant's Chemical works of St. Rollox. Although this also became the railway workshops' official name, every generation, even to this day, simply called them the 'Caley'. In the 1923 Railway Act, the Caledonian was grouped into the London Midland & Scottish Railway Company and the building of locomotives ceased in 1928 with just repair and maintenance work continuing. Another name-change occurred in 1948 (British Railways) and in 1971 the railway workshops became part of British Rail Engineering Ltd. finally ceasing as such in 1987.

The Caledonian Railway Locomotive No.'721' was the first of the 4-4-0 "Dunalastair" class in an initial order of fifteen, built at the Company's St. Rollox works in 1896. "Dunalastair" was the name of the Perthshire estate belonging to the Caledonian Railway's Chairman — James C. Bunten. The locomotive's designer was John Farquharson McIntosh, their Locomotive Superintendent who improved and modified further orders until his retirement in 1914. These engines were strongly constructed, had low maintenance costs and many survived into the nationalisation of British Railways.

Behind the tenements opposite the Caley was Huntingdon Place and this was their street-team. Huntingdon F.C. was well supported during the depression and their ground was Fountainwell Park, levelled off from soda waste dumped there by St. Rollox Chemical Works for years. The Sighthill housing estate now covers this area. This is the 1931 line-up on the occasion of the West of Scotland Intermediate Cup played at 'Old' Saracen Park where the 'Hunts' beat local rivals Springburn United in the Final after two replays:

Secretary McGeoch, Edgar, Smith, Trueman, Clark, Baggaley, McFadyen
Howard?, Burke, Student, Black, Bell.

St. Rollox U.F. Church FC Churches League Champions.

All grades of football were played in the district — Schools, Churches, Amateur, Juvenile, Junior and even Senior!! When the Scottish League was formed in 1890, an original member was Cowlairs and another early club was Northern F.C., but professionalism and the lack of ground facilities had caused their extinctions by 1896.

The Churches League Secretary for years was Jimmy Budd of Gourlay St. and prominent local teams were St. Rollox, Cowlairs Parish, and Kenmure Men's Own. In this league foul tackles could be overlooked, but never foul language.

The most notable monument in this cemetery is that of Andrew Hardie of Glasgow and John Baird of Condorrat, the 1820 Radical Rising Martyrs who were executed at Stirling Castle for treason. The name of James Wilson of Strathaven, another weaver executed at Glasgow on the same charge, was added at a later date.

Other notable gravestones are to Benjamin Connor, Superintendent Engineer of the 'Caley', architect William Leiper, landscape painter John Milne Donald, sculptor John G. Mossman and violinist Mackenzie Murdoch, composer of 'Hame O' Mine'. His Iona Cross Memorial was unveiled by Sir Harry Lauder in 1924.

8

The Cunarder tramcar on route 25 to Bishopbriggs shooglies its way past the 'Coffin', the nickname given to the Kinema, erected in 1926 on the site of a former one, Canadian Picture House, but known to all by its number in High Springburn Road — "The Three Nineteen". The Kinema closed in 1958 and the ground is now landscaped, complementing the new housing around. The Co-op building on the right still survives and is looking good, as are the refurbished tenements in Keppochhill Road, seen here in the background.

9

REV. GEORGE HANSON.

REV. WILLIAM KEIR.

SIGHTHILL CHURCH

REV. H. H. AITCHISON

REV. WILLIAM HERON.

This commemorative card celebrates the Diamond Jubilee (1872-1932) of Sighthill Church, which was situated at the corner of Springburn Road and Mollinsburn Street. The years of service for the ministers depicted were 1872-1923 (Rev. Hanson), 1912-1927 (Rev. Keir), 1927-1931 (Rev. Aitchison) and 1931-1951 (Rev. Heron). The next minister was Rev. John H. Prendergast, from 1951 to 1978, when the congregation, already united with Cowlairs Sommerville, joined with others to become Springburn Parish. They now worship in a newly built church at Springburn Way and Atlas Road. The service of Dedication was on 14th May 1981.

10

Springburn Road, Springburn.

The area around here of Mollinsburn and Adamswell Streets was the playground for two distinguished writers and television personalities — Molly Weir and her brother, Tom. On the left was the Fire Station, a famous landmark for directing strangers to Springburn — "See the fire station, get off at the next stop for the Prince's" or "Two stops after the station is the Co-op" and so on. Beyond Keppochhill Road there were tenements and shops on both sides right up to Hawthorn Street. This was the real selling place for the housewives on shopping sprees, often determined to purchase goods here rather than go into town.

11

PETERSHILL F. C.

Left to Right, standing: D. Rutherford (Trainer), A. Sommerville, J. Cadden, R. Henderson, G. Nisbet, J. Rutherford, A. Patrick, W. Livingston (Ass^t Trainer); sitting: D. Croal, C. Sutherland, J. Young (Captain), R. Sim, J. Mc Kim.
1915——1916 Winners of Scottish Cup, Glasgow Charity Cup & Maryhill Charity Cup.

"Easy the Peasy" is the terracing chant from the supporters of Petershill Juniors F.C. and so it should be. During this 1990-91 season they scored their 10,000th goal in competitive games. They have also been League Champions ten times and have won the Scottish Cup on five occasions. The last time was on Saturday 19th May 1956 when the 'Peasy' beat Lugar Boswell Thistle 4-1. Mr. D'Angostini, the owner of Prince's Cafe in Gourlay Street gave the district's children free ice cream 'pokey hats' for the honour of displaying the Cup in his shop window.

12

Petershill Park's football pitch, terracing, pavilion and dressing rooms were all executed by voluntary labour in the 1930s. The central terracing was also covered by volunteer workers in the late 1950s. The opening game, in 1935, was a friendly between Celtic and Rangers with an attendance of 28,000 including Lord Provost Sir Alexander Swan who officially opened the Park. Petershill F.C. was founded in 1897 and their first ground was Arrol Park which is now part of Cape Insulation Boards. The next was Atlas Park (1903) and this was the site for the 'Mons' factory in 1914. Hawthorn Park was their last ground before returning to Petershill Road.

Fire Station, Springburn

This station cost £4,000 and took 18 months to build, being ready in August 1893 with married quarters for ten firemen. The building stood at the corner of Springburn and Keppochhill Roads, but the expressway has made this a busy crossroads so a replacement was constructed at Petershill Road in 1986. The old station was converted into flats, each selling at a fixed price of £28.250.

Springburn's most discussed fire was on New Year's night in 1941, when the Oxford Picture House was burned down, the most remarkable fact being that the cinema was next door to the Fire Station.

14

From early 1890 Springburn folk were campaigning for a suitable hall, large enough to accommodate their festivals, soirees and functions. One of the bitterest opponents to this was Baillie Samuel Chisholm who, at the laying of the memorial stone declared, "Springburn is the petted and spoiled child of the Corporation". It was ironical that as Lord Provost he officially opened the Public on 16th May 1902. The architect was William B. Whitie who also designed the Public Library. Unfortunately, the building is now in a derelict condition and only the proposal by the Springburn and Possilpark Housing Association for a Business Centre seems the likely one to save the Public.

The Edinburgh and Glasgow Railway opened on 21st February 1842, but it could have been a few years earlier if the proprietors of the Forth and Clyde Canal had allowed the railway to bridge across it on its way into Glasgow. This refusal meant tunnelling underneath it very steeply into Queen Street terminal. To assist ascending trains, a rope was attached to the front and hauled up by a stationary winding engine, housed at Cowlairs. On the descent, all trains stopped at Cowlairs and brakevans were coupled on to enable a safe arrival. Many wee boys believed that the train going downhill pulled the one coming uphill. Banking engines took the place of the winding one in 1908.

The Edinburgh and Glasgow Railway Company decided that their main engineering works would be sited at Cowlairs, so called after the lands and mansion taken over by them. In 1865 the company was bought over by the North British, the largest Scottish railway and five years later, Cowlairs became the biggest railway works in Scotland. In the 1923 Railway Grouping, the North British became part of the London and North Eastern Railway and continued as such until the 1948 nationalisation into British Railways. Twenty years on, the works were closed down and only the Glasgow to Edinburgh main line is still in existence, while the rest has become the Cowlairs Industrial Estate.

The general store at 341 Springburn Road, next to Hoey's, was well known as Lizzie McFarlane's, but in 1911 this was the grand entrance into the Springburn Electric Theatre, the district's first cinema. Later this was renamed the Ideal, (nicknamed 'Bug-Hut'), and finally the Royal.

When these premises changed to the Oxford Billiards Hall, entry was through the closemouth of 339, as 341 was converted into a shop. The next occupier was Andy Roberts, the bookmaker, and the halls were finally used for Prize Bingo. In the 1970s, the tenements were knocked down to make way for a new expressway.

For nearly a hundred years, the big family store in Springburn was Samuel Hoey's. He started in a shop with two windows and a staff of two and expanded into an emporium with thirty-six windows and a staff of sixty. Selling almost everything, there was no need to go into town — "Hoey's would have it", be this clothing — fashionable or industrial, crockery — earthenware or china, furniture — domestic or stylish, carpets and wedding gifts. For the children there would be toys, books and games abundantly displayed weeks before Christmas and all prices had to be keen to compete with their local rivals — Cowlairs Co-operative and their huge dividend.

SPRINGBURN CROSS.

At Vulcan Street corner the Cowlairs Co-op celebrated their 21st anniversary by installing this granite fountain in August 1902. The Society was formed by a group of North British railwaymen from Cowlairs and the first shop was opened on 20th August 1881. At the end of 1901 there were 4,394 members, sales amounted to £196,561 and there were 26 branches.

The Saturday following the unveiling was a Gala Day for 6,000 children who paraded with bands and banners to Springburn Park. At the end of the celebrations, each child was presented with a commemorative mug.

Transferring Walter M. Neilson's engineering works from Hydepark Street, Anderston to Springburn, was masterminded by his manager Henry Dubs by 1862. One year later, Dubs and others had left and started the Glasgow Locomotive works in the southside. Neilson recalled a former manager, James Reid, to be his managing partner.
In 1876, Reid bought out Neilson and continued to expand into the home and export markets. By 1892, he had brought four of his sons into the business and renamed it Neilson Reid & Co. His eldest surviving son, Hugh, was responsible for amalgamating the three locomotive manufacturers in Glasgow into the North British Locomotive Company in 1903.

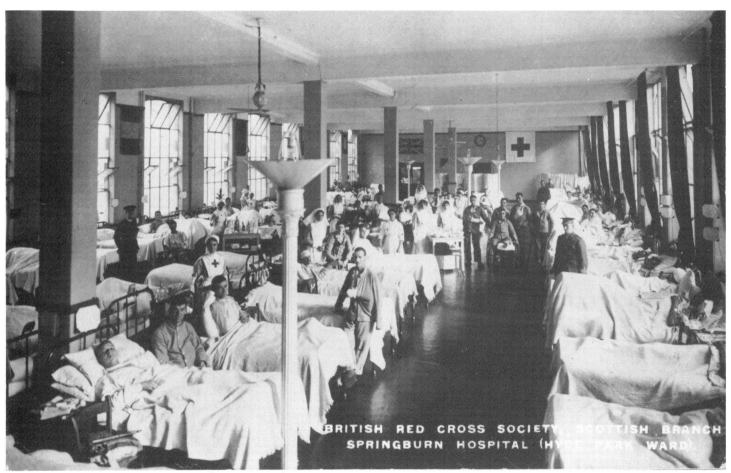

BRITISH RED CROSS SOCIETY, SCOTTISH BRANCH
SPRINGBURN HOSPITAL (HYDE PARK WARD)

In 1914 large numbers of wounded soldiers and sailors were brought home from the War fronts and hospital accommodation was proving to be inadequate. The North British Locomotive Company's Board of Directors offered the main portion of their Administrative Building to the Scottish Branch of the British Red Cross. Known as the Springburn Hospital, with the entrance in Adamswell Street, the total capacity was 400 beds placed in five large wards aptly called Hyde Park, Atlas, Queen's Park, Victoria and Springburn. These were ready by Christmas Eve 1914 and by the closing day on 21st May 1919 the nursing staff and doctors had attended to 8,211 men.

BRITISH RED CROSS SOCIETY SCOTTISH BRANCH,
SPRINGBURN HOSPITAL (QUADRANGLE).

Convalescent soldiers, relaxing with nurses and orderlies, pose for this photograph. A set of these photos, showing also the building and wards, was given to King George V, who expressed through Sir Frederick Milner that he was pleased that such valuable work was being done by the Red Cross in Glasgow.

Sir Frederick, after a re-visit in 1916, wrote, "I was more charmed with Springburn than ever, and give it first prize of all the hospitals I have seen, it is quite perfect, and the men seem so happy and contented."

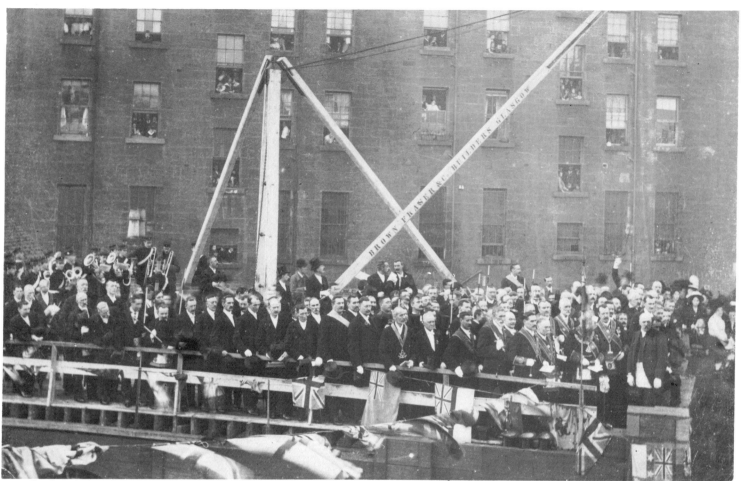

The laying of the foundation stone 1909 of the Masonic Halls for Lodge Kenmuir, numbering 570 in the Roll of the Grand Lodge of Scotland, was a gala occasion for many local men. Captain Speirs of Elderslie, Provincial Grand Master, performed this duty with due pomp and ceremony. The Springburn Silver Band was also in attendance whilst an uninvited audience watched interestedly from the back-court windows facing into Vulcan Street. Today the Halls and the Library are the only ones remaining as the street was bi-sected when the new Atlas Road was formed as the entry to Springburn.

A Hyde Park built locomotive destined for the Malayan State Railways awaits in Vulcan Street for traffic clearance and police escort to Stobcross Quay where the big crane will load the engine onto a Clan or a City liner, bound for the Far East. Such an event created a carnival atmosphere and excitement amongst children and housewives looking from windows, backcourts and closes. Often the transportation took place after midnight when the trams had stopped running and traffic was light. Even at this late hour, the same keen interest would be shown by watching locals.

The Cross, Springburn

From early morning, hereabouts would be crowded with workmen shuffling noisily with their hob-nailed boots to clock onto the workshops of Cowlairs and Hyde Park. Later, housewives would be scurrying uphill, trailing zinc baths on wheels or pushing prams laden with clothes, to try to catch their 'turn' at the steamie. By mid-day, others would be shopping for groceries and bargains whilst proud mothers would be perambulating with babies in the afternoon. After 5 o'clock, the workmen would be hashing homewards and a couple of hours later the populace would be turning out for entertainment at the pictures or the dancing.

Springburn Road, Glasgow.

The message on this postcard, sent on 26th July 1906, reads: "Do you recognise the old place? The clothing shop which you see on the right hand side, is at the corner of that new road which was opened when you were last here and used to be known as the 'Smithy Road'. This leads away out to the 'Atlas'. It is now called 'Station Road' and is almost immediately opposite Springburn Station."

Because of the duplication of many street names in Glasgow, this changed to Atlas Street and when re-aligning of new roadways was completed in 1983, it was again altered to Atlas Road and is a principal thoroughfare.

ATLAS ENGINEERING WORKS, SPRINGBURN

Walter Montgomerie Neilson returned to Springburn in 1884 to establish the Clyde Locomotive Works directly opposite his former Hyde Park works (see page 21). Orders were not readily forthcoming and in 1888 he sold out to Sharp Stewart & Co., who had been building locomotives since 1834 at their Atlas Works in Manchester. The Springburn works were given the same name and their main gate was in Edgefauld Road. Two large sheds, built at the outbreak of the Great War, were used for manufacturing munitions and weapons and named after that war's first two battles — 'Mons' and 'Marne'.

Audiences of over 2,000 often attended summer concerts in the park. Popular bands of the first quarter of this century were the Springburn Sons of Temperance, Springburn Silver Prize Band, Springburn Rechabite Reed Band and the North British Locomotive Works Silver Band, which would include members from their Queen's Park, Atlas and Hyde Park works. They practised in the quadrangle of the Administrative Building. Perhaps the best known band up until urban redevelopment was the Salvation Army Silver Band, which marched from Flemington Street to their Citadel in Wellfield Street every Sunday.

SPRINGBURN PARISH CHURCH.

This church was the first in Springburn and the last of twenty churches planned by the Glasgow Church Building Society in 1841. It was first known as Springburn Hill Church because of its situation at the top of Hill (later Hillkirk) Street. The Service of Dedication was on 3rd May 1842.

Springburn Parish was the last parish in Glasgow to be created under the New Parishes (Scotland) Act of 1844 when it was disjoined from the Barony of Glasgow on 14th June 1854 and hence the church was renamed Springburn Parish Church. In 1899, the church was enlarged with the addition of two deep transepts. It was united with Springburn North Church in 1967 and again changed name, this time to Springburn North Hill. In 1978, it was united with others and is now part of the new church in Atlas Road.

30

In Hillkirk Street is Saint Aloysius' Chapel, the oldest surviving place of worship in Springburn, erected in 1881-82 to the designs of J.R. Bruce and incorporating the east end of an earlier (1856) chapel. The High Altar was by Pugin and Pugin, the main architects to the Diocese.

A plaque, donated by the parishioners, staff and children of Saint Aloysius' school, was unveiled by Archbishop Winning in 1982 to celebrate Saint Aloysius' centenary and to commemorate that year's visit to Glasgow by Pope John Paul II.

Avenue Road, Springburn.

In spite of a name-change to Northcroft Road in the early 1920s, even up to the tenements' demolition in the 1970s this place was always known as 'The Avenue'. Cornering off to the right was another street, which has almost gone in the area's redevelopment for a new shopping centre. This was Wellfield Street and a popular place in it was the Springburn Picture House, better known as the 'Wellie' or 'Wellfield', which closed down in 1960 as the 'Astor'. Another building of local interest was the Salvation Army Citadel. A new one is now at the corner of Hawthorn and Fernbank Streets.

Springburn Road looking North. This scene hardly changed for nearly three-quarters of a century, but what a difference now! Today, the tenement building on the left between Carleston Street and Kay Street is all that remains. Gone are Kay Street Baths, the 'Steamie', the 'Swings', tramcars and the traffic.

In 1989, the Parks and Recreation Department opened a newly built Sports Centre on the site of the old recreation grounds, but it lacks one essential amenity — a swimming pool! Fronting the centre is a larger than life athletic statue in fibreglass entitled 'The Bringer', sculptured by Andrew Scott and erected in April 1991.

These two storey houses in Springvale Place were demolished in 1909 and the ground was levelled off to the main road. The area became a children's playground with robust equipment and a little park which had a white tiled fountain in the middle. There was also an old men's club where board games such as draughts, chess and dominoes could be contested in a room full of smoke from thick black plug tobacco and clay pipes.

BALGRAY RECREATION GROUND, SPRINGBURN.

This playground, known locally as the 'Swings', lasted until the early 1980s when new roads, pathways and a sports centre took the place of the grounds and fountain which were gifted to the populace in 1911 by Hugh Reid of the North British Locomotive Company.

Part of the Springburn North Church can be seen at the right and to the side of this the ropewalk of the local Ropeworks. At the top left are the 'Blocks' erected in 1863 by the Edinburgh and Glasgow Railway Company to house their workers as part of a planned model village. Unfortunately, no further developments were completed due to financial difficulties. The houses were demolished in 1967.

Springburn Road (Car Terminus).

This scene can only invoke memories, for all these well-kent landmarks are now gone. Springburn North U.F. Church was built in 1890 and was situated at the corner of Springburn Road and Elmvale Street. In March 1967, it united with Springburn Hill. The vacant church was vandelized and destroyed later in the same year.

At the opposite corner of Elmvale Street was Maguire's Pub and above this were the Argyll Halls used for social functions and dancing. Later, when the pub was Healy's Terminus Bar in the 1960s, the Halls became their singing Lounge. A decade later, the owner was ex-Celtic and Hibernian footballer Chris Shevlane, who now has premises elsewhere in Springburn.

Balgray Hill, Springburn.

The bottom of the Balgray was the most popular choice for photographers in the postcard publishing business. The building featuring the clock was Quin's, one of the best loved public houses in the district. Their Balgrayhill entrance had a small bar and a games room whilst 'underneath the stairs was the wee room', now immortalized in song. Doorways to this and the main bar were in Springburn Road and in front of Quin's was the tram shelter. Another long established hostelry was Gemmell's, which ended up as the Kelvin. The church, Wellfield United, was erected in 1899 and in 1978 united with others to form Springburn Parish Church. Only the Barclay Street tenement at the hilltop remains.

HAWTHORN STREET, SPRINGBURN.

There were very few streets off Springburn Road which did not have a pub at one corner or the other. Hawthorn Street had two in Edwardian times; on the north side, The Boundary — 'the first and last bar' at this end of the city and on the other side was Smith's. Next to this was a dairy, Miller's, who had other shops in the district, all advertising their handmade bread at 5½d per 4lb loaf with a further ½d off if the customer bought sides and ends.

The new Boundary Bar of 1937-1938 was designed by James Weddell and William Beresford Inglis, the Art Deco architects responsible for Glasgow's first skyscraper hotel, the Beresford, in Sauchiehall Street.

The lounge bar was reached from Springburn Road, but the entrances to the off-sales and huge bar were in Hawthorn Street. Inside were seated alcoves, but these were categorically for men only and used for domino playing. Transport themes were etched on windows and several of these were of Stephenson's Rocket. The Boundary was considered the best 'howff' in Springburn and is still sadly missed and fondly remembered.

Elmvale School. Springburn.

Inside the old wards of Cowlairs and Springburn were eight elementary schools — Albert, Elmvale, Hyde Park, Keppochhill, Petershill, Saint Aloysius, Springburn (known as Gourlay Street by locals) and Wellfield.
Keppochhill and Petershill were demolished whilst Albert and Saint Aloysius were completely rebuilt and are the main intakes of the Primaries. Of the four remaining buildings, only Elmvale survives as a Primary; the others are utilized for community purposes.

The Last Car for Springburn

The first electrically driven tramcars in Glasgow ran between Mitchell Street and Springburn, the inaugural service being on 13th October 1898. After witnessing the trial trips, one old dear was reported to have said, "Ah hiv seen caurs pulled by horses, ah hiv seen them gaun by cable, but ah never thoc't ah'd see the day when a caur wid be pulled by a fishin' rod."

Comic postcards with the local place-name overprinted were widely available and popular in Edwardian times and the new tramcars were a sufficient novelty to be lampooned, as in this example by Cynicus (Martin Anderson).

The last tramcar for Springburn was the number 18 route coming via Shawfield, withdrawn on 3rd June 1961.

SPRINGBURN PARK, GLASGOW.

The Corporation of Glasgow bought the lands, 58 acres in total, of Mosesfield and Cockmuir for £25,000. They were laid out as Springburn Park to the plans of A.B. McDonald, City Engineer, in 1892. Later, the 20 acres of New Mosesfield were added. The highest point of the park is 351 feet above sea level. Due to the steepness of Balgrayhill, Springburn was the only park in Glasgow which didn't have a tramcar service to the gates.

The bandstand was gifted by James Reid in 1893. It was manufactured at the nearby Saracen Foundry of Walter McFarlane and Company.

REID'S MONUMENT, SPRINGBURN PARK, GLASGOW.

In October 1900, the 'St. Rollox and Springburn Express' launched a fund for a memorial to James Reid, respected citizen and Springburn's greatest industrialist. The bronze statue of Reid, sculpted by Gascombe John and standing 1½ times life-size on a granite plinth, was unveiled on 3rd October 1903 by ex-Lord Provost Sir James Bell. Three plaques represent his terms of office as President of the Society of Engineers and Shipbuilders, President of the Royal Glasgow Institute of Fine Arts and as Lord Dean of Guild.

The inscription reads: 'James Reid of Auchterarder and Hyde Park Locomotive Works. Born 1823. Died 1894.'

BOWLING GREEN, SPRINGBURN PARK, GLASGOW.

On Wednesday 16th August 1905, Lord Provost Sir John and Lady Ure Primrose officially opened the public bowling greens. Mrs. Marion Reid of Belmont rolled a silver jack and the first bowl to the accompaniment of cheers. She retained the jack as a memento of the occasion. The greens are still kept in excellent playing condition and much used. The district once had four other public greens at Cowlairs Park and also two private clubs — Cowlairs in Hillkirk Place and Springburn in Broomfield Road. Only the latter, established 1858, still exists.

Springburn was one of four Glasgow public parks which could boast a cricket pitch and this was well used by this Cowlairs XI. Perhaps their best remembered match was the charity one against "Sir" Andrew Dougall's XI. He was a colourful character and was also known as the "Earl of Hogganfield".

So great was the interest in cricket in 1893 that there were discussions about forming a league championship amongst the district's clubs, which were Belmont, Springburn, Union and two quaintly named ones — Ravenna and Gonzaga.

James Duncan, who in 1820 was a book-seller and publisher in the Saltmarket, had New Mosesfield House built in 1838 for his bride. He married late in life and a year after his death, his widow was alarmed by the entry of two burglars who fled when she confronted them with a double-barrelled shotgun. Shaken by this experience, she decided to take up residence elsewhere and the house was then vacant for some time.

The next occupant was the minister (1861-1895) of Springburn United Presbyterian Church, the Reverend James Aitchiston Johnston in whose honour the church was subsequently renamed as the Johnston Memorial Church.

Mosesfield Museum, Springburn Park, Glasgow

Reverend Johnston's son George was an inventor. At Mosesfield in 1896, he designed and constructed the mobile dog-cart which put Scotland on the automobile market when he became co-founder of the firm which was to become the Arrol Johnston Company.

In 1904, Hugh Reid purchased the lands and the mansion of New Mosesfield and gifted these to the Corporation as an addition to Springburn Park. He suggested that the upper floor be used as a house for the Park Superintendent and the ground floor be open to the public as determined by the Parks Committee. This became a museum and then an old men's club as it still is today.

Belmont, Springburn.

As Glasgow's highest house, this handsome mansion had magnificent outlooks across the city and beyond into seven counties. The villa was built in 1888-89 for Hugh Reid and his bride Marion Bell (the daughter of a wealthy shipowner). Hugh was the second son of James Reid of Hyde Park works. In 1903, the locomotive manufacturers of Glasgow amalgamated to form the North British Locomotive Company and Hugh became their first managing director. He was knighted in 1922.

48

DUCK POND.   SPRINGBURN PARK.

This view of Belmont shows extensions (1901 and 1908) and the grounds adjoining Springburn Park and Stobhill Hospital. When Sir Hugh died in 1935, he bequeathed the mansion to the hospital for use as a children's home in memory of his wife Marion, who had died in 1913. The Marion Bell home was later used as training and living quarters for nurses and as Administrative Rooms for the Board of Management.

Unfortunately they decided to demolish this fine edifice in 1985 because of repeated vandalism, fires and high security costs. All that remains are the two red sandstone pillars of the lodge gates. This is now an auxiliary entrance to Stobhill.

Stobhill was built as a Poor Law Hospital by the Parish Council. First planned in 1899, it was fully operational by the time of the formal opening in September 1904. At a Springburn Ratepayers Meeting in February 1904, Parish Councillor Miller stated in his annual report that the cost would be about £250,000 and that Stobhill would be guaranteed to be one of the showpieces of Glasgow.

This aerial view shows sports grounds in the foreground which became the greatly needed and splendid New Theatre Suite, first proposed in 1960 and completed in 1970.

Immediately after the outbreak of the Great War, Stobhill was requisitioned by the Royal Army Medical Corps for wounded servicemen. This became known as the 3rd Scottish General Hospital under Colonel Hay and the 4th Scottish General Hospital under Colonel Napier. A staff of 240 nurses were needed to administer care to the wounded and as early as September 1914, over 200 men had been admitted. Eventually, there was a full complement of 1,040 patients to be treated daily and this continued until the end of 1919. By the spring of 1920, the hospital had returned to civilian use.

A SELECT BIBLIOGRAPHY

Canning, Rt. Rev. Bernard	The Living Stone: St Aloysius' Church 1882-1982. John S. Burns & Sons, 1982
Glasgow Corporation	Leisure in the Parks. Official handbook of 1974
Herron, Very Rev. Andrew	Historical Directory to the Glasgow Presbytery. unpublished mss, 1984
North British Locomotive Company	Commemorative 1914-18 book

St. Rollox and Springburn Express 1893-1908

Springburn Museum Trust	Springburn Heritage Trail, 1988
Springburn Reminiscence Group	You Must Remember This. Springburn Museum Trust, 1990
Thomas, John	The Springburn Story. David and Charles, 1964.
Watt, Oliver M.	Stobhill Hospital — the first seventy years. University Press, Glasgow, 1971

ACKNOWLEDGEMENTS

I should like to acknowledge my thanks to Ms. Alison Cutforth, Curator of Springburn Museum for her permission to reproduce a few photographs and postcards which were not in my collection and also to Ms. Susan Scott, Designer and Photographer, for her assistance.

I would recommend to anyone who may have memorabilia of Springburn to contact the very co-operative staff of the Museum (041-557-1405). They would be very pleased to receive or copy such material for their ever increasing collection.

My thanks are also given to Bob Rae, my colleague from Strathclyde Postcard Club, for the loan of his "Caley" postcard and to a stalwart of Springburn, Douglas McMillan, for his contribution.

52